YOUR KNOWLEDGE HAS VALUE

- We will publish your bachelor's and master's thesis, essays and papers

- Your own eBook and book - sold worldwide in all relevant shops

- Earn money with each sale

Upload your text at www.GRIN.com
and publish for free

Bibliographic information published by the German National Library:

The German National Library lists this publication in the National Bibliography; detailed bibliographic data are available on the Internet at http://dnb.dnb.de .

This book is copyright material and must not be copied, reproduced, transferred, distributed, leased, licensed or publicly performed or used in any way except as specifically permitted in writing by the publishers, as allowed under the terms and conditions under which it was purchased or as strictly permitted by applicable copyright law. Any unauthorized distribution or use of this text may be a direct infringement of the author s and publisher s rights and those responsible may be liable in law accordingly.

Imprint:

Copyright © 2004 GRIN Verlag, Open Publishing GmbH
Print and binding: Books on Demand GmbH, Norderstedt Germany
ISBN: 9783668344143

This book at GRIN:

http://www.grin.com/en/e-book/343568/the-wild-geese-by-mori-ogai-a-hybrid-literary-artifact

Ian Akbar

"The Wild Geese" by Mori Ogai. A Hybrid Literary Artifact?

GRIN Publishing

GRIN - Your knowledge has value

Since its foundation in 1998, GRIN has specialized in publishing academic texts by students, college teachers and other academics as e-book and printed book. The website www.grin.com is an ideal platform for presenting term papers, final papers, scientific essays, dissertations and specialist books.

Visit us on the internet:

http://www.grin.com/

http://www.facebook.com/grincom

http://www.twitter.com/grin_com

Is Mori Ogai's *The Wild Geese* a hybrid literary artifact?

The Meiji period from 1868 to 1912, in Japan, was a time of rapid adoption of Western/European styles, products and practices in an attempt to be more modern. Indeed, it appears that according to Varley (2000: 71/72), the terms 'Western" and 'modern' were thought of as synonymous. Accordingly, Mori Ogai's *The Wild Geese* is representative of that particular historical period; the transition from the Tokugawa period (1603 – 1867) to the Meiji period (1868 – 1912), and therefore by definition can be considered an artifact of that period insofar as it consistently, as will be demonstrated, presents examples of this particular historical period. In addition, in terms of hybridity, which is defined as something heterogeneous in origin or composition (Merriam-Webster Online 2004), this paper will also illustrate that this novel possesses elements of both the Japanese and the Western novel, of the time, and, therefore, can properly be referred to as a hybrid literary artifact.

In the Japanese literary tradition, before Meiji, the novel was referred to as the *shosetsu* or *shi-shosetsu* which loosely translated means 'I novel'. Starrs (2000: 150) points out that it was a form of self-confession which was very different from the structure of the western novel. Basically, according to Starrs (2000: 147), the central character was used as an alter ego for the author himself. In *The Wild Geese*, Okada (one of the main characters) is obviously representative of Ogai himself. In one case in particular the relationship is clear. Kato (1979: 128) mentions that in 1884, when he was twenty-two, Ogai went to Germany to study hygiene, returning to Japan four years later. In the novel, a Leipzig University professor takes Okada [to Germany], who is also a young man, and helps him pass his doctoral examinations. (Ogai 1959,

113) Of course, opportunities to go and study abroad were a new feature brought on by contact with the West and Europe during this time.

The incident involving Ogai travelling abroad points to another feature of the author's life we find in *The Wild Geese*; his adoption of the characteristic of resignation. Since Ogai was a doctor in the Japanese army, he had no choice but to go to Germany. He simply had to accept it. Correspondingly, according to Miyoshi (1974: 180), for the character Okada, the offer of the overseas job took, his growing relationship with Otama (another central character), out of his hands. We do not know if Ogai also was involved in a relationship with a woman before he left for Germany. However, due to Kato (1979, 128/129), we do know that Ogai was in love with a German woman who followed him to Japan, but due to the responsibilities placed on him as eldest son in his family, he denied the woman and his love for her. This occurrence illuminates the importance of resignation for Ogai. Miyoshi (1974: footnote 172) points out that due to the fact that Ogai had no choice but to accept certain situations in his own life, resignation became Ogai's favourite motto in life. This resignation is manifested in the novel when Otama learns of Suezo's (the man who purchases Otama to be his mistress) profession and again when Okada leaves Otama behind. (Ogai 1959, 47/118) Thus, both Okada and Otama serve to illustrate an important feature of the author's life.

One of the most glaring similarities between Ogai and Okada is their having the same facilities in written Chinese and spoken German. When Okada mentions that a German professor was looking for a student who could read Chinese and also speak German, Ogai is of course referring to himself. As is mentioned by Kato (1979: 128) in *A History of Japanese Literature*, Ogai possessed a thorough knowledge of classical Chinese and also spoke and wrote German. Therefore, by Ogai using features of his own life as a source of inspiration or model, he is at the same time demonstrating a central feature of the Japanese novel of the time, the *shosetsu*.

Another similarity exists between the apparent feelings of the narrator and Ogai himself regarding the West and Japanese practices. Some changes during the Meiji Era, which were incorporated into *The Wild Geese,* were inspired by Western standards of appearance which were considered more civilized. As mentioned in the novel, 'the wheeled stall vanished from its set place under the eaves. And the house and its surroundings, which were always modest, seemed suddenly attacked by what was then fashionably called "civilization," for new boards over the ditch replaced the broken and warped ones, and a new lattice door had been installed at the entrance.' (Ogai 1959, 23) It appears that the disappearance of the wheeled stall, the placement of new boards and a new door were all attempts to be or appear more 'civilized'. However, the narrator seems to be skeptical as to how necessary these changes were, which would accord with the fact, as Starrs (2000: 137) notes, that Ogai became a staunch supporter of things Japanese later in his life.

This sentiment continues when the narrator mentions that 'some years later the area around the [Shinobazu] pond was ruined and made into a race track (presumably for horses), and then again, by one of those unusual transformations of the world, into a bicycle track.' (Ogai 1959, 33) The narrator, who again is representative of the author himself, seems to be iterating that it was a tragedy to attempt to change the area around the Shinobazu pond into a racetrack when he uses the word 'ruined'. The racetrack apparently did not last. He then refers to 'those unusual transformations of the world' by which he seems to be referring to progress, causing yet another manifestation of the Meiji period to be built, a bicycle track. (Japan Cycling Federation 2001) In the end, the author appears to be lamenting the fact that the area around a beautiful pond was sacrificed in the name of progress for what he feels was no good reason. These passages directly reflect a strong similarity between the feelings of the narrator and Ogai himself.

The *shosetsu* was also, according to Starrs (2000: 151) characterized by many beautiful passages. Accordingly the reader's pathos is aroused when in such passages as when Otama begins to take interest in Okada. 'When Okada takes off his cap and greets her for the first time, her heart seems to lift, and she feels herself blushing.' (Ogai 1959, 77/78) And, again, after Okada destroys the snake, Otama contemplates how to send him a thank-you. 'At that moment Okada came by with his usual greeting. 'Red to the ears, Otama stood bolt upright with the broom in her hand, but she let him walk on without saying a word.' (Ogai 1959, 95) Otama continues to contemplate what to do until she finally decides on a course of action. She makes elaborate preparations, only to be disappointed. As the narrator states, she was transformed as she fixed her eyes on Okada. 'When he took off his cap, I noticed how upset he was, and I saw him unconsciously quicken his step.' (Ogai 1959, 109) The scene describing the wild geese themselves is also very evocative. (Ogai 1959, 110) These passages generate feelings of hope, expectancy, sympathy, sorrow and appreciation in the reader. They are undoubtedly, touching

According to Miyoshi (1974: 175/176) another feature of the Japanese novel is unexplained changes in the narrative (i.e., first to third person), which are accounted for by the Japanese sentence form which allows omission of the subject. Miyoshi (1974: 156) also mentions that the grammatic person shifts around very freely from first to third, and from one first-person speaker to another first-person speaker. Therefore, the narration can shift from the third-person novel to the first-person diary, confession, or letter. In addition Miyoshi (1974: 175) draws attention to the fact that in *The Wild Geese*, the narrator, Okada's friend, begins by reminiscing on past events, but soon disappears from the tale, almost making it a third-person story. He returns in Chapter 18 when it becomes increasingly clumsy to present events which the narrator cannot have been in a position to know. This is, however, very representative of the Japanese form of storytelling which is exemplified in the *shosetsu*.

In contrast, as mentioned by Starrs (2000: 136/140), the defining features of the Western novel, of the time, were that it was usually book length (i.e., longer than a short story), it celebrated nationalism in a positive way, had a large cast of characters and was not so much a personal account of the day to day lives of the characters but more of an epic tale where heroes and villains were larger than life. *The Wild Geese*, definitely conforms to the first criteria, being over 100 pages, it could hardly be referred to as a short story. It does not, however, appear to celebrate nationalism in a positive way. Such references to Okada going abroad to improve his qualifications; it being his one concession to the way of the world suggests that personal/professional improvement cannot be obtained in Japan. (Ogai 1959, 114) It does, however, seem to have a large cast of characters (i.e., Okada, Suezo, Otama, Otama's father, Otsune, the children, Ume, etc.) and as explained by Miyoshi (1974: 157), the characters in the Japanese novel are almost always types, and not living individuals. Therefore, by definition, the characters of *The Wild Geese* are representatives of types of Japanese people and can therefore be considered to be larger than life, insofar, as many of Japan's people have known situations and relationships of the type represented in Ogai's work. In short, it would seem that this work seems to include three of the four criteria of the Western novel, in addition to the characteristics of the traditional Japanese novel, and consequently can be correctly referred to as a hybrid novel.

Now we turn to an examination of how Western and traditional Japanese practices, styles and products are manifested within *The Wild Geese*. In order to accommodate change during this time previous structures were utilized, e.g., when Lord Todo's estate was turned into a student dormitory. The author goes on to compare the window style of the old estate with that of a new one. 'Its windows, of vertical wooden bars as thick as a man's arms, were set at wide intervals in a wall of gray tiles plastered in a checkerboard fashion. Of course you can't see windows like those now except in the castle turrets of the emperor's palace, and even the bars of the lion and tiger cages in the Ueno Zoo are more slenderly made than those were.' (Ogai 1959, 21) Of course, the bars on the windows of a Tokugawa era estate belonging to a samurai, as well as the Emperor's Palace would need to be thick and strong as protection against attack. However, in the Meiji era, the bars on the windows of the Ueno Zoo (1882, to the present) (Asian Info.org, 2000) became much more slender, no doubt because they were made of steel.

In addition, the police box is mentioned when Okada, the narrator and Ishihara are attempting to pass with Ishihara carrying the dead goose under his clothing. (Ogai 1959, 116/117) Apparently, the police box, which has become ubiquitous in Japan since Meiji, has its origins, according to Seidensticker (1983: 95), in certain Edo practices, but just as probably began with the guards at the gates of the legations and the foreign settlements. The closest settlement at that time to Edo, which is modern day Tokyo, was Yokohama. Seidensticker (1983: 98) also mentions that the military and the police were the first to go Western in terms of uniform and dress, emphasizing the importance of Western fashion. This circumstance is also illustrated in *The Wild Geese*.

In the novel, a storekeeper is mentioned as having a cropped head of hair. (Ogai 1959, 24) And, as was stated above, Okada had a fondness for wearing a cap. (Ogai 1959, 19/20) The cap was a Western contrivance, which was very popular during the Meiji era. Of course, wearing of a cap was only possible when one had a cropped head of hair. Haircuts were also a very popular item during this time. Varley (2000: 75) points out that it was the Japanese military who first cut their topknots in order to wear the hats of their Western-style uniforms. Accordingly, Seidensticker (1983: 94) mentions that a cropped head was considered synonymous with 'Civilization and Enlightenment'. To complete the analysis, from top to bottom, the police also took to wearing Western style shoes. (Ogai 1959, 23) It would appear that the individuals and groups of this time incorporated substantial amounts of Western dress and fashion into their comportment which *The Wild Geese* accurately reflects.

Moreover, student uniforms of the Western style, as Seidensticker (1983: 102) notes, were also adopted for men in mid-Meiji, and so came the choke collars and the blackness relieved only by brass buttons that prevailed through the Second World War. In the novel, Ishihara is mentioned as a young man wearing a student's uniform standing at the water's edge and watching something. (Ogai 1959, 110) In addition, Varley (2000: 74) mentions that during the 1870s, Western clothes, deemed more practical and up-to-date, were increasingly worn by men in the cities, often combined amusingly with items of the native costume. In the novel, a woman enters during a theatre intermission with a companion wearing a *yukata* and a panama hat. (Ogai 1959, 43) Furthermore, Seidensticker (1983: 91) points out that even in the years of the deepest Tokugawa isolation there had been foreign fads, such as one for calicos, originally brought in as sugar sacks, and later much in vogue as kimono fabrics. Accordingly, in *The Wild Geese*, Otama is mentioned taking a calico apron from a bag of imitation leather. (Ogai 1959, 47)

Of particular importance to the story is when Suezo decides to buy some vividly coloured linnets for Otama, the Western influence is again present. He also notices cages of parrots, parakeets and imported canaries hung high on the eaves and white doves and Korean pigeons on the floor. (Ogai 1959, 82/83) The linnets which are purchased along with a cage are clearly representative of Suezo keeping Otama as his mistress. But, due to Otama's growing dissatisfaction and growing awareness, it appears that their relationship will be short-lived. Sooner or later, as Miyoshi (1974: 177) explains Otama will have to fly from her cage. Thus this passage serves to epitomize the Japanese cultural fascination with fleeting, temporary things (i.e., cherry blossoms, etc.).

Equally of importance to the story is the presence of a parasol. The parasol was first introduced to Japan in the Tokugawa period. (Eras of Elegance, Inc., 2000-2003) The parasol, in the novel, is bought in Yokohama by Suezo for his wife. It is obviously of Western make. It is described as being all right for a tall foreigner to toy with. Suezo, however, buys Otama the same parasol, which Otsune discovers upon seeing her with it. (Ogai 1959, 64) When Otsune does see Otama with the parasol which is unsuited to her, she remarks how different it is from hers. (Ogai 1959, 65) This discovery of duplicity on Suezo's part sparks a confrontation between Suezo and

Otsune which he deflects by claiming he is being unjustly persecuted. Suezo claims that the parasol is probably available in Ginza (Ogai 1959, 70), which is an area in central Tokyo which continues to import all the latest upper class trends and fashions to this day.

Naturally, during this time, many practices of the past were in decline. In regards to tradesmen, *The Wild Geese* is explicit when it refers to the fact that 'As late as the second decade of Meiji era [1878 to 1888], the customs of the tradesmen's houses in Edo were still kept up, although they were slowly dying out." (Ogai 1959, 104) Also, in the novel, it is mentioned that 'the other man was an engraver who had remained at the old craft in spite of his fellow-craftsmen's having abandoned the trade in order to make seals.' (Ogai 1959, 99) Seals were historically handmade and were therefore engraved. With the birth of this new era they began to be mass produced, by machine. (Lutterbeck 2000, 4) No doubt, some craftsmen left their traditional occupations to take part in these changes and the profits they generated.

Lastly, the novel also refers to the existence of magazines as the *Kagetsu Shins*hi, which printed the first translation of a Western novel. (Ogai 1959, 16) Indeed, at this time Western/European novels were only beginning to be translated into Japanese. The first of such translations, due to their ease, were children's stories. The narrator draws a comparison between such a story and the present one, which is not of importance to this analysis, but again draws attention to the importance of Western/European influences on this work. (Ogai 1959, 107) However, Japanese translations of Chinese literature have a far greater history than those of the West. Therefore, seeing Ogai's expertise in Chinese, it is not surprising to find consistent references to the influence of China in Japan, especially in *The Wild Geese*. (Ogai 1959, 85) Otama is even compared to the heroine in the Chinese novel the *Kimpeibai*. (Ogai 1959, 92) It is, however, unknown how much of an influence this novel had on the writing of the present work. Although, if Chinese influences were to be found interwoven within its construction, that would further serve to support *The Wild Geese's* claim to that of hybrid literary artifact.

As has been demonstrated, Mori Ogai's *The Wild Geese* is replete with examples illustrating the social conditions during the transition from the Tokugawa period to the Meiji period. These examples have highlighted the importance of Western product influences and social practices, as well as, the physical changes brought about by Japan's attempt to modernize during the Meiji period. These examples, have also demonstrated that *The Wild Geese* can be aptly referred to as a literary artifact. In addition, Ogai's novel having conformed to most of the criteria denoting a Western novel and all of those concerning the Japanese novel, the *shosetsu*, in accordance with a definition of hybridity as being of heterogeneous composition, can also be described as a hybrid novel. Therefore, it is with great confidence that this paper concludes that Mori Ogai's *The Wild Geese* is indeed a hybrid, literary artifact, and, thus is worthy of serious examination and further study by all connoisseurs of historical fiction, students of literature, and anthropologists interested in the history of the Japanese novel and in this Japanese historical period.

Bibliography

Asian Info.org, 2000. 'Places to visit in Tokyo'. Retrieved on September 23, 2004 from http://www.asianinfo.org/asianinfo/tokyo/places_to_visit_in_tokyo.htm

Eras of Elegance, Inc., 2000-2003, 'Eastern and Western Artistic Styles Throughout History'. Retrieved on September 23, 2004 from http://www.erasofelegance.com/august2001_art.html

Japan Cycling Federation, 2001. 'History of the Bicycle and Bicycle Racing'. Retreived September 22, 2004 from http://www.jcf.or.jp/eng2/history/

Kato, Shuichi, 1979, *A History of Japanese Literature* in CIJ 421: Cultural Contact and Hybridity in the Arts in Asia, Resource Book. University of New England, Armidale, NSW. pp. 107-116 and 133-149, inclusive.

Lutterbeck, Bernd, Ishii, K and Gehring, Robert A, 2000, 'Governing Legal Identities, Lessons from the Histories of Seals and Signatures'. pp. 2 – 11. Retrieved on September 23, 2004 from http://ig.cs.tu-berlin.de/oldstatic/ap/rg/2000-09/ISSE_Paper_Gehring_etal.pdf

Merriam-Webster Online, 2004. Retrieved September 9, 2004 from http://www.m-w.com/cgi-bin/dictionary?book=Dictionary&va=prolifically

Miyoshi, Masao, 1974, *Accomplices of Silence* in CIJ 421: Cultural Contact and Hybridity in the Arts in Asia, Resource Book. University of New England, Armidale, NSW. pp. ix-xviii and pp. 38-54.

Ogai, Mori. 1959, *The Wild Geese*, Tuttle Publishing, Singapore.

Seidensticker, Edward, 1983, *Low City, High City* in CIJ 421: Cultural Contact and Hybridity in the Arts in Asia, Resource Book. University of New England, Armidale, NSW. pp. 1983: 90-109.

Starrs, Roy, 2000, 'In search of the great Meiji novel'. In: *Coloniality, postcoloniality and modernity in Japan* in CIJ 421: Cultural Contact and Hybridity in the Arts in Asia, Resource Book. University of New England, Armidale, NSW. pp. 197-218.

Varley, Paul, 2000, *Japanese Culture* (4th edition) in CIJ 421: Cultural Contact and Hybridity in the Arts in Asia, Resource Book. University of New England, Armidale, NSW. pp, 235-256 (excerpt from 'Encounter with the West')

YOUR KNOWLEDGE HAS VALUE

- We will publish your bachelor's and master's thesis, essays and papers

- Your own eBook and book - sold worldwide in all relevant shops

- Earn money with each sale

Upload your text at www.GRIN.com
and publish for free